ABOUT THE BOOK

W ith a moving Preface by Maureen and John Sheehan, Co-Presidents of Corpus USA, this book tells the sad story of how, in the eleventh century, the so-called papal "Gregorian Reform" forcibly imposed "clerical celibacy" on traditionally married Western male Catholic bishops and presbyters (priests).

To that end, Gregorian popes drove bishops' and priests' wives out of their Christian homes and forced many into homelessness, prostitution, or suicide. They forced other bishops' and priests' wives – along with their children – into slavery, including in the papacy's Lateran Palace.

The Gregorian campaign constituted a cruel attack on the thousand-year old apostolic tradition of Catholic married bishops and Catholic married presbyters – a tradition rooted in the New Testament. For example, the Epistles of First Timothy (3:2-5) and Titus (1:5-7) required that bishops and presbyters should be "*married only once*," and be good fathers to their children.

The popes of the "Gregorian Reform," inspired by a spiritual misogyny infecting some networks of Benedictine monasticism, tried by police power to smash that ancient apostolic tradition in the Western Church. Behind their attacks stood their ruthless ambition to construct a papal theocracy by means of a celibate cadre.

Their campaign tragically precipitated an institutional battle between heterosexual bishops and priests on one side, and homosexual bishops and priests on the other, with homosexual priests found especially in monasticism. Yet the book sees that battle as indeed tragic, since "clerics" on both sides were brothers equally beloved by God.

In addition, the book contextualizes the "Gregorian Reform" within a wide span of three historical stages in the social construction of the modern Western male "clerical-celibate-seminary model" of the Catholic episcopate and presbyterate:

- *Stage 1 - late classical construction of the "clerical state,"* imported from the Roman pagan priesthood in the fourth century for the new organizational model of the Imperial Church;

- *Stage 2 - 'high' medieval construction of "clerical celibacy,"* cruelly imposed in the eleventh-century "Gregorian Reform" by the papal lust for theocratic power, and inspired by misogynist spiritual corruptions within Benedictine monasticism;

- *Stage 3 - early modern mandate of clerically segregated seminaries,* decreed by the Council of Trent in the sixteenth century, in order to resist Protestantism by protecting "seminarians" within a monastic-like environment.

Today, this book argues, the modern Western male "clerical-celibate-seminary" model of the presbyterate and episcopate is breaking down. It has become sociologically dysfunctional and evangelically counter-productive.

Finally, the book proposes that, in response to that breakdown, the Holy Spirit is now inspiring a lay-centered postmodern "New Evangelization," energized especially by postmodern feminine spiritual regeneration.

THE CRUEL ELEVENTH-CENTURY
IMPOSITION OF WESTERN CLERICAL CELIBACY

A Monastic-Inspired Papal Attack
On Catholic Episcopal & Presbyteral Families

JOE HOLLAND
(www.joe-holland.net)

Preface by Maureen & John Sheehan
Co-Presidents, CORPUS-USA
(www.corpus.org)

Adapted and expanded from excerpts of the author's book titled
POSTMODERN ECOLOGICAL SPIRITUALITY
(Pacem in Terris Press, 2017)

PACEM IN TERRIS PRESS

Devoted to the memory of Saint John XXIII,
founder of Postmodern Catholic Social Teaching,
and in support of the search for a Postmodern Ecological Civilization
seeking to learn from the ecological-spiritual wisdom traditions
of our entire global family.
(www.paceminterrispress.com)

ISBN-13: 978-0999608807
ISBN-10: 0999608800

Cover photo from Wikipedia's
Article of Gregory VII at
https://en.wikipedia.org/wiki/Pope_Gregory_VII

Corrections made on 2018-0-14

With gratitude to
Maureen & John Sheehan for the Preface
and to Art Kane for proofreading the text

PACEM IN TERRIS PRESS
is the publishing service of

PAX ROMANA
Catholic Movement for Intellectual & Cultural Affairs
USA

1025 Connecticut Avenue NW, Suite 1000,
Washington DC 20036
(www.paceminterris.net)

TABLE OF CONTENTS

PREFACE

MAUREEN & JOHN SHEEHAN

Co-Presidents, CORPUS USA

(http://www.corpus.org)

M any Catholics often refer to the "vow" of celibacy for Western diocesan clergy. In fact, there is no "vow." It is a requirement dating back to the eleventh century that became part of the Canon Law of the Western or Roman Catholic Church. The Eastern Churches never agreed to mandatory celibacy.

In addition, not many people are aware that compulsory "clerical celibacy" for the Western diocesan clergy was originally imported from monasticism and imposed against an apostolic tradition. For the first thousand years of the Church's history, most Catholic bishops and priests (or presbyters) were married and had families, as was presumed in the New Testament.

But, in the eleventh century, that all changed in the Western Church.

By police force and vicious attacks, the papal "Gregorian Reform" imposed compulsory "clerical celibacy" on married Catholic bishops and priests. The attacks on their wives and children were often more vicious.

Pope Gregory VII (1073-1085), after whom the "Gregorian Reform" is named, demanded that all Western married bishops and presbyters abandon their wives and children. That brutal campaign broke up families, and often displaced wives to homelessness, prostitution, slavery, and suicide.

With great detail, Dr. Joe Holland traces that eleventh-century imposition of "clerical celibacy," and how it sought to create a separate celibate clerical caste that would be loyal to the pope and solidify papal power.

Holland skillfully weaves a picture of the historical buildup, and the contemporary breakdown, of the clerical, celibate, and seminary-trained model for the Western Catholic priesthood, and how that model has now become an obstacle to the Holy Spirit's call for a "New Evangelization."

There are some interesting jewels sprinkled throughout the text. One is the story of Irish-Keltic monasticism. Highly educated Irish-Keltic monks travelled all over Europe to convert the migrating Germanic tribes.

Irish-Keltic Christianity, centered in its distinct form of monasticism, celebrated salvation as embracing Nature and welcomed the leadership of strong women – with male and female monasteries in Ireland often led by female abbesses. However, Irish-Keltic monasticism was replaced by St. Benedict's Latin monasticism, which later helped to restore imperial consciousness within the Latin Church.

At the present time, Keltic eco-spirituality has re-emerged as an eco-spiritual response to the global ecological crisis. In that regard, Holland describes Peter Maurin's call for a new lay agroecological monastic movement as modeled on Irish-Keltic monasticism.[1] Recovering eco-spiritual roots in "Mother Earth," this model represents an important strategic response to the vast devastation of life's integral ecology.

As we witness climate change and global warming, Modern Industrial Civilization has become spiritually, humanly, and ecologically unsustainable. In response, Dr. Holland proposes that:

> *Undoing that clericalizing, monasticizing, and educationally segregating model for the diocesan presbyterate will prove to be one regenerative seed for the sustainable development of a future Postmodern Ecological Spirituality, a future postmodern "New Evangelization," and a future Postmodern Ecological Civilization.*

---

[1] Peter Maurin (1887-1949) was co-founder with Dorothy Day of the Catholic Worker Movement.

1

INTRODUCTION

T he content of this small book is partially excerpted and further developed from my larger book titled POSTMODERN ECOLOGICAL SPIRITUALITY.[1]

I have separated out and expanded the material in this small book because not everyone who is interested in the issue of "clerical celibacy" may be also interested in the wider range of reflections found in that larger book.

In addition, having the material available in a small book makes it more available to the global movement promoting the end of mandatory "clerical celibacy" in the Western or Roman Catholic Church.

---

[1] Joe Holland, POSTMODERN ECOLOGICAL SPIRITUALITY: CATHOLIC CHRISTIAN HOPE FOR THE DAWN OF A POSTMODERN ECOLOGICAL CIVILIZATION RISING FROM WITHIN THE SPIRITUAL DARK NIGHT OF MODERN INDUSTRIAL CIVILIZATION (Pacem in Terris Press, 2017).

Note that the book does not use the word "postmodern" in the common academic meaning, which implies Relativism or even Nihilism, since that understanding is (in my view) only late modern. Rather, it uses the word "postmodern" to indicate a new era in human history that seeks a regenerative Postmodern Ecological Civilization.

In that larger book POSTMODERN ECOLOGICAL SPIRITUALITY, I explored historical-spiritual dimensions of what I call "The Great Postmodern Transition." That is the transition out of the breakdown of Modern Industrial Civilization and into the search for a regenerative and democratic Postmodern Ecological Civilization.

In terms of that transition, that book argues that the *late modern global breakdown of life's "integral ecology"*[2] is precipitating the foundational breakdown not only of Modern Industrial Civilization, but also of what I call "Modern Psychological Spirituality," both of which are Western in origin.

Further, that book proposes that such a broad social-analytical framework is also needed to understand the correlative breakdown, at least in the 'advanced' industrialized nations, of the modern Western strategy of Catholic evangelization. That breakdown includes the related breakdowns of the modern Western "apostolic" model of "religious life and of the modern Western "clerical-celibate-seminary" model of the presbyterate (priesthood) and of the episcopate.[3]

---

[2] The phrase "integral ecology," meaning holistic ecology, is take from Pope Francis' 2015 encyclical, LAUDATO SI' – ON CARE FOR OUR COMMON HOME, available as a pdf file at: *http://w2.vatican.va/content/dam/francesco/pdf/encyclicals/documents/papa-francesco_20150524_enciclica-laudato-si_en.pdf (accessed 2017-10-02).*

[3] Following the New Testament, this book uses the term "presbyter" rather than the later usage of the word "priest."

The book does not address the parallel crisis of the Western Catholic episcopate, since that would require its own full study. The crisis of the episcopate is not as obvious as the crisis of the presbyterate, since there seems to be a surplus of career-oriented Western Catholic presbyters pursuing a "vocation" to the episcopate. In addition, according to the latest institutional reports, while the number of Catholic presbyters in the world has decreased, the number of Catholic bishops has increased.

This small book provides an historical framework for understanding the breakdown of the modern Western "clerical-celibate-seminary" model of the Catholic presbyterate within 'advanced' industrialized nations, and *especially for understanding the dysfunctionally non-evangelical character of "clerical celibacy."*

It also sees that breakdown and dysfunction as key historical-spiritual dimensions of the wider breakdown of the five-hundred-year-old bourgeois project of the West's "Modern World."[4]

As this small book will explain, in the eleventh century the so-called "Gregorian Reform" imposed "clerical celibacy" – by force – on diocesan bishops and presbyters across the Western Church, and in so doing destroyed their Catholic families.[5]

That forced imposition of "clerical celibacy" on Western bishops and presbyters caused bitter anger in the Eastern Churches, and it aggravated the continuing eleventh-century schism between the Western or Roman Catholic Church and what are today the Eastern Orthodox Churches. Centuries later, the legacy of that forced imposition also contributed to the success of the division in Western Christianity known as the "Protestant Reformation."

---

[4] The analysis of the breakdown of the "Modern World" (and within it of Modern Industrial Civilization), as found in my book POSTMODERN ECOLOGICAL SPIRITUALITY, is partly inspired by the now classic 1950 text by the German-Italian Catholic philosopher, Romano Guardini, THE END OF THE MODERN WORLD, Revised Edition (ISI Books, 2001). Pope Francis, in his great encyclical on ecology LAUDATO SI', cited Guardini's book eight times.

[5] For more on this history from early efforts to impose "clerical celibacy" before the "Gregory Reform," during it, and up to the Council of Trent, see Chapter 2 of the late Capuchin prophet Michael H. Crosby's excellent study, CELIBACY: MEANS OF CONTROL OR MANDATE OF THE HEART? (Ave Maria Press, 1996). He later followed that book with a sequel titled RETHINKING CELIBACY: RECLAIMING THE CHURCH (Wipf & Stock Pub, 2003).

There were scattered efforts early in Christian history to demand celibacy for bishops and presbyters, especially by zealot-like Christian monks influenced by extreme Platonism, or in some cases by Marcionism or Manichaeism. They tended to view sexual intercourse as "impure," even in marriage, and they frequently held misogynist views of women.

As monasticism (not of apostolic origin) gained power, some zealot-like monks became bishops, and they tried to use local or regional church councils to advance their campaign. But the first truly ecumenical council, held at Nicaea in 325, rejected their sectarian drive for mandatory celibacy.

Although the Ecumenical Council of Nicaea protected the apostolic tradition, some zealot-like monk-popes subsequently again tried to impose celibacy on diocesan presbyters and bishops. But their non-evangelical distortion never took root.

Prior to the "Gregorian Reform," the apostolic tradition of married bishops and presbyters held across East and West throughout the *first millennium* of Christianity. After that, throughout the *second millennia* of Christianity, the Eastern Churches continued to reject the imposition of "clerical celibacy" on diocesan presbyters.

Now, in the early years of the *third millennium* of Christianity, the Eastern Churches, both Orthodox and Catholic, continue (with minor exceptions) their ancient apostolic tradition of married presbyters.

Today, since the modern historical-spiritual form of the Western Catholic presbyterate is so clearly breaking down, there should be no need any longer to argue that reality. But it is important to understand *the deep roots of that breakdown*. In order to do so, we need first to remember the foundational "lay" nature of the original spiritual-prophetic movement that Jesus founded, which we call "Church."

Original "Way" of Jesus as Lay

The brutal Roman Empire crucified Jesus – who had chosen the role of a Jewish lay teacher (rabbi) and prophet – as a political threat to the Empire. The Empire also subsequently executed Peter and Paul, both Jewish laypersons, as well as thousands of other Christians, all of whom were lay.

That foundational Christian period has been called the "Age of Martyrs," since the Empire executed so many Christians for following the "Way" of Jesus.

Throughout the Apostolic Era and for several centuries after, Christianity remained *exclusively lay*. In that foundational era, there was no such thing as the "religious state in life" (with "state" meaning status or class). Nor was there any such thing as the "clerical state in life."

Early on, there emerged disciples who were ordained for authority-bearing offices (deacons, presbyters, and bishops), as well as disciples with special charisms for the community (including communities of virgins and widows). Yet all were lay.

Again, in the church's early centuries, those offices and charisms did not represent separate "states-in-life." There was originally only *the one lay "Way" of the baptized,* including for ordained lay leaders and lay disciples with special charisms. There was only the "Way" of Jesus' own lay path.

The word "lay" comes from the Greek word *Laos,* which means "people." In the Greek Septuagint translation of the Hebrew Scriptures and in Greek texts of the New Testament, *Laos* means the holy, royal, priestly People of God. Further, in the New Testament, the Greek work *kleros* (from which we get "clergy") means "chosen." The New Testament uses the word *kleros* to signify that everyone within the *Laos* of Jesus' disciples is "chosen."

Thus, the contemporary canonical "clerical state" (again, with the word "clerical" coming from the Greek word *kleros*) is not a constitutive dimension of the Church. It did not exist in the foundational early centuries of Christianity. It is also based on a misinterpretation of the New Testament's use of the Greek word *kleros.*

Further, the Catholic tradition came to understand Baptism, Confirmation, Ordination, and Marriage as "sacraments" (along with other sacraments). But the canonical "clerical state" is not a sacrament. Even so, in the Western Catholic Church at least, it often became elevated in practice above the "laity," and thus above the sacraments of Baptism, Confirmation, and Marriage.

Nonetheless, within its late classical historical context, the "clerical state" represented an inculturation for that historical stage of Christianity. It later carried over into medieval and modern forms. But, again, clericalism was not part of the original "Way" of Jesus' lay path.

Institutional Obstacles
to a "New Evangelization"

Today, I propose that, as we enter what I call "The Great Postmodern Transition," the still-functioning late-classical social construction of the "clerical state," and the still functioning high-medieval forced imposition of "clerical celibacy," have both become *institutional obstacles* to the Holy Spirit's call for a postmodern "New Evangelization."

10

I also propose that the modern Western Catholic seminary-system of "clerical education" – generally segregated from Catholic universities and from the wider Catholic laity – has also become an *institutional obstacle* to the "New Evangelization."

Again, this small book proposes that, in the late modern period of the Western Catholic Church, the "clerical state," mandatory "clerical celibacy," and the segregated clerical-celibate seminary system, have all become institutional obstacles blocking the Holy Spirit's call for a postmodern "New Evangelization."

The central analysis of this small book, however, is how "clerical celibacy" was cruelly imposed by police-force during the eleventh century on traditionally married Catholic bishops and diocesan presbyters. But, in order to better understand that imposition of "clerical celibacy" in its fullest context, this book pursues the following historical steps.

- *Foundational Apostolic Tradition.* The study begins by reminding us of the apostolic tradition of episcopal and presbyteral families, which continued in the Western Catholic Church for a thousand years – throughout the entire first millennium of Christianity – and continues today with married presbyters and presbyteral families in both the Eastern Catholic Churches and the Eastern Orthodox Churches, as well as in the Western-rooted Protestant Churches.

- *Fourth-Century Creation of the "Clerical State."* Then, the study traces the oldest roots of the contemporary breakdown of the modern form of the Western Catholic presbyterate to the late classical imperial construction of the "clerical state." which separated the "clergy" from the "laity," set the "clergy" to rule over the "laity," and thus introduced a non-evangelical hierarchical dualism into the single "*Laos*." (Note that the non-

11

evangelical word "hierarchy" is still widely used as a name for bishops – so strong is its dualistic legacy.)

- *Two Stages of Western Feudal Monasticism.* Next, the study sketches the two-stage feudal development of Western medieval monasticism: first Irish-Keltic and then Benedictine-Latin. A later development of the second stage provided inspiration for the misogynist and theocratic papal campaign to impose "clerical celibacy" by police force on traditionally married Western Catholic bishops and diocesan presbyters.

- *Papal Attack on Episcopal & Presbyteral Families.* After that, the study narrates the cruel and vicious papal attacks by the monastic-inspired "Gregorian Reform" on the families of traditionally married Western Catholic bishops and diocesan presbyters.

- *Postmodern Implications.* Finally, the study reflects on some contemporary implications of that legacy for church and society within "The Great Postmodern Transition" from Modern Industrial Civilization to Postmodern Ecological Civilization.

Let us now recall the ancient apostolic tradition of Catholic married bishops and presbyters, and its roots in the New Testament.

2

APOSTOLIC TRADITION OF
EPISCOPAL & PRESBYTERAL FAMILIES

J esus' first public miracle was for a wedding feast, and he appears to have chosen mostly married individuals as his apostles. Similarly, the episcopal and presbyteral leaders of the Apostolic Church were generally married.

That apostolic tradition of episcopal and presbyteral families continued in the Western Latin or Roman Church *for more than a thousand years of Christian history*. During that period, Western bishops and diocesan presbyters typically were family people, that is, they had wives and children. Thus, family life was the typical background of candidates for ordination.

Further and as noted, after more than two thousand years of Christian history, most presbyters in practically all the twenty-three non-Roman and *sui-juris* Catholic Churches (all in full communion with the Catholic Bishop of Rome) are married to Catholic women and have Catholic children.

In those non-Roman Catholic Churches, diocesan presbyters who do not marry are often called "monastic priests." But that is a euphemism, since they typically do not belong to monasteries.

We find in the New Testament the earliest written witness to the apostolic tradition of bishops and presbyters having families. The Epistles of First Timothy and Titus presumed that bishops and presbyters overseeing the communities of Jesus' disciples were married and had children. Thus, I TIMOTHY 3:2-5 states:

> *Therefore, a bishop must be irreproachable, **married only once**, temperate, self-controlled, decent, hospitable, able to teach, not a drunkard, not aggressive, but gentle, not contentious, not a lover of money. **He must manage his own household well, keeping his children under control with perfect dignity**; for if a man does not know how to manage his own household, how can he take care of the church of God? (Bold font added.)*

Similarly, TITUS 1:5-7 states:

> *Appoint presbyters in every town, as I directed you, on condition that a man be blameless, **married only once, with believing children** who are not accused of licentiousness or rebellious. For a bishop as God's steward must be blameless, not arrogant, not irritable, not a drunkard, not aggressive, not greedy for sordid gain. (Again, bold font added.)*[1]

Having a successful marriage and well-managed children was thus a typical expectation for ordination in apostolic times and beyond. Certainly, there were exceptions like St. Paul, who never married. But, as noted, being married and having children was

---

[1] The above biblical quotations are from the NEW AMERICAN BIBLE. Note that, in the early church, bishops and presbyters were not clearly distinguished.

the common situation for bishops and presbyters for the first thousand years of the Western Catholic Church.

In addition, as also noted, in practically all the Eastern Orthodox Churches and Eastern Catholic Churches, as well as in the Western-rooted Protestant Churches, presbyters are still today typically married.

Over against the perhaps hundreds of medieval and modern Western Catholic theological volumes defending the eleventh-century papacy's cruel and forced imposition of mandatory "clerical celibacy" on its bishops and diocesan presbyters, the clear teaching of the New Testament and the clear practice of the Apostolic Church, as well as the ancient and continuing witness of the Eastern Catholic and Orthodox Churches, at least for diocesan presbyters, must rank higher.

3

IMPERIAL CONSTRUCTION OF
THE NON-EVANGELICAL CLERICAL STATE

End of Persecuted Lay Church
& Rise of Imperial Hierarchical Church

In the early fourth century of the first Christian millennium, Roman imperial leaders saw the lay movement of Christianity – already spreading rapidly throughout the Empire – as offering the possibility of holding together the externally threatened and internally disintegrating imperial society.

As external attacks by migrating 'barbarian' Germanic tribes intensified and as the Empire began to degenerate internally, the Christian movement appeared to imperial leaders to offer unifying organizational strength. That was because the Christian cosmopolitan vision was not limited to any specific geographic, ethnic, or class identity.

From the time of the fifty-seventh Roman Emperor, Constantine the Great (272-337), ruling from Constantinople (formerly Byzantium) in what is today's Turkey, the imperial government constructed an ecclesial-political alliance with the Catholic bishops of the imperial regions (then called "dioceses").

The Roman Empire, which had crucified Jesus and probably thousands of his followers, appealed to the episcopal leaders of Jesus' disciples in the desperate hope of saving itself. Most bishops accepted the invitation, though the Coptic Church of Africa resisted imperial take-over and continued to suffer persecution from the Imperial State in its new partnership with the new imperial model of the Christian Church.

That acceptance soon led to Christianity becoming the official religion of the Empire, reshaped by imperial consciousness, and backed by the coercive power of the Imperial State.

Within that profound ecclesial-societal shift, the first history of the Catholic Church, written by the Catholic bishop Eusebius of Caesarea (c. 263-339), who was close to the imperial household, described the Emperor Constantine ruling on his throne as reflecting an imperial image of God.[1]

To strengthen that fourth-century episcopal-imperial alliance, the Emperor Constantine gave to the Catholic-Christian bishops in many towns an imperial building for their gatherings. The Greek word for emperor is *basileus*, so those imperial buildings were called (in English translation) "basilicas," meaning buildings of the Emperor. Imperial basilicas thus became the first large church buildings.

---

[1] See EUSEBIUS: THE CHURCH HISTORY, transl. Paul L. Maier (Kraeger, 2007). Note that, contrary to GENESIS 1:27, the image does not include woman.

Prior to that gift of imperial buildings, the community of Jesus' disciples had typically gathered during three centuries for the Lord's Supper in *people's homes*. Following the donation of imperial buildings to the bishops, a tendency emerged to think of the "Church" as *holy buildings* (so today we "go to Church"), rather than as the sacred community of Jesus' disciples who form the holy, chosen, and priestly *Laos*.

Significance of
the Imperial Construction

Further, with the new alliance between the Catholic bishops and the Empire, imperial leaders extended to the bishops and to their presbyters the *special class-rank of the imperial pagan priesthood*. That special imperial class-rank is the pagan legal origin of the "clerical state" (again, with "state" meaning "status").

That imperial "state" legally gave to Jesus' ordained disciples *certain government-granted economic and political privileges, which Jesus' non-ordained disciples did not receive* – for example, exemption from imperial taxes and from military service in the imperial army, plus a legal court only for those in the "clerical state."[2]

Again, the Greek word *kleros*, from which the word "clergy" is derived, refers in the Greek texts of the New Testament to the

---

[2] The "clerical state" and the sacrament of ordination are distinct entities. The contemporary Western Catholic canonical requirement of "clerical celibacy" is linked not ontologically to ordination but only juridically to the invention of the "clerical state." For that reason, an ordained "clerical-celibate" presbyter in the Roman Catholic Church may be released from the obligation of "clerical celibacy" by "reduction to the lay state." Yet even after that "reduction" or "laicization," the individual remains ontologically an ordained presbyter. But, by Canon Law, he is no longer a member of the "clerical state" and as a "lay person" is forbidden to function as a presbyter, despite his still valid ordination.

"chosen" character of all disciples of Jesus who form the holy *Laos* (1 Peter 2:5-10).

Yet in a non-evangelical manner, the New Testament's lay term *kleros* became misidentified with a 'higher' "clerical class" ruling from 'above' the *Laos* of Jesus' non-clerical disciples. As a result, a non-evangelical tendency also emerged to identify clericalized bishops and presbyters as "*the Church*," rather than the full *Laos* of all Jesus' disciples.

That Constantinian episcopal-imperial alliance then geographically expanded the Christian evangelization of Western Civilization. It often did so, however, through military force imposed on 'uncivilized' (meaning not living in cities) European tribal peoples.

During the second millennium of Christianity, that same violent process continued to be inflicted on 'uncivilized' non-European tribal peoples, who were conquered by European mercantile colonialism and still later and more broadly by European and European-American industrial colonialism.

Along with its contributions, that late classical Greco-Roman episcopal-imperial alliance created *three anti-evangelical distortions* of the original apostolic community of Jesus' disciples.

- **Loss of Lay Identity.** First, it weakened the foundational evangelical truth that Christian Church is entirely a "lay" (again, from the Greek word *laos*) and "chosen" (again, from the Greek word from *kleros*) community of Jesus' disciples. It did that by promoting a wrong sense that the church was a state-sponsored institution identified with set of *temple-like buildings,* and alternately with a *hierarchical "clerical class,"* receiving state

20

privileges that the rest of Jesus' lay and chosen disciples did not receive.

- **Ruling Clerical Class.** Second, it weakened the foundational evangelical command that the ordained leaders of Jesus' disciples were to function as *servant-leaders* of the wider lay community. It did that by social construction of an imperially privileged "clerical class" empowered by the imperial state to *rule hierarchically over the Laos.*

- **Cross as Imperial Military Conquest.** Third, since many now clericalized church leaders supported the militaristic Roman Imperial State, a hierarchical-patriarchal and military-command style of leadership was imposed on the Catholic community.

That military-imperial style for ecclesial leadership undermined the foundational evangelical doctrine of *the Cross as a symbol of persecution.* That undermining not only legitimated imperial, class-based, and gender-based domination. It also inverted the meaning of the Cross *from Jesus' non-violent suffering of execution by the Empire to episcopal-support for the Empire's violent conquest of tribal peoples.*

As a symbol of that third distortion of Christianity, we have the legend of Constantine seeing in a vision the Cross of the non-violent Jesus with Greek words that have been traditionally rendered in Latin as *"In hoc signo vinces"* (under this sign you will conquer). Thus was the prophetic meaning of the Cross of Jesus inverted. Again, no longer a symbol of *imperial persecution,* the Cross became disfigured as a symbol of *imperial conquest,* and in the name of imperial Christian Civilization.

Again, that imperial identification of evangelization with imperial violence would continue for Western Catholic Christianity through to the time of the modern European-*Christian genocidal conquest of the Original Peoples of the Americas*. It also included the hundreds of years of the *torturous and murderous Atlantic Slave System*, with many Catholic "religious orders" and many bishops holding slaves.

Again, it later evolved during the late nineteenth and early twentieth centuries into *Modern Western Industrial Colonialism*. Catholic examples of Modern Western Industrial Colonialism included Catholic Belgian King Leopold's personally held "Congo Free State," which caused the unjust killing of perhaps ten-million people, as well as the twentieth-century 'imperial' conquest of Ethiopia by the officially 'Catholic' Italian and papally endorsed fascist state of Benito Mussolini.

Predominantly Protestant modern examples included the vast British Empire across Africa, Asia, and the Caribbean, as well as the United States' genocidal military attacks on the First Nations of the continent – most infamously in the Cherokee "Trail of Tears." It also included Modern Western Neo-Colonialism throughout Africa, the Asian/Pacific region, and the Latin American/Caribbean region. "Cross and sword" (and later machine gun) thus continued in Western partnership into the twentieth century.

Three Steps in Social Construction
of the Modern Western Catholic Presbyterate

To understand the breakdown of the modern Western model of the Catholic presbyterate, we may now discern three important historical steps in its social construction.

Again, in the fourth century, the Catholic-Christian episcopacy and presbyterate had been "clericalized" by the Roman Empire's Constantinian construction of the Imperial Church. Later in the eleventh century, the "Gregorian Reform" imported its papal law of celibacy from Benedictine monasticism and cruelly imposed it by police-force on traditionally married Western Catholic diocesan presbyters and bishops.

Still later, at the sixteenth-century Ecumenical Council of Trent, the modern Western presbyteral model of education was consolidated in a manner again analogous to monasticism. A decree from the Fifth Session of the Council required special schools for standardized training of future priests. Called "seminaries" and deliberately separated from universities and from the "laity," these schools imitated monastic life.

The immediate purpose of this monastic segregation of "seminarians" was to combat Protestantism's penetration through kinship networks into European-Catholic regions. Yet this segregation uprooted Catholic evangelization from its traditional roots, dating back to apostolic times, in local kinship and friendship networks.

In addition, following the Council of Trent, Western Catholic bishops tried even more intensely to enforce monastic-inspired celibacy upon their diocesan presbyters, though not always with success.

Again, there have been three distinct historical stages in the sociological construction of what I have called the modern Western "clerical-celibate-seminary" model of the Catholic presbyterate, which is now breaking down.

- *Stage 1 - Imperial Clericalism.* In the fourth century, the Emperor Constantine legally 'elevated' bishops and presbyters to a 'higher' imperial class authorized to rule over the "laity," with laity then demoted below "clergy" in the new and non-evangelical hierarchical structure of the Imperial Church.

- *Stage 2 - Monastic Celibacy.* In the eleventh century, the papal 'Gregorian Reform,' inspired by the Benedictine monastic network of Cluny, imposed monastic celibacy through police-force on traditionally married Western diocesan bishops and presbyters, in order to construct a clerical-celibate theocracy.

- *Stage 3 - Monastic Seminaries.* In the sixteenth century, the Council of Trent decreed that candidates for the diocesan presbyterate should be educated in monastic-like "seminaries" outside universities, and in ecclesial segregation from the rest of the priestly *Laos*.

By contrast, the Protestant Reformation rightfully rejected the non-evangelical papal law of monastic celibacy for Western Catholic diocesan presbyters and bishops, and it successfully launched its still-continuing wave of global evangelization.

The Reformation's rejection of that papal law was one of the reasons for the Reformation's initial successes in Northern Europe, since so many Catholic presbyters at the time maintained 'illegal' common-law marriages with children. It must certainly also be one of the major reasons for the continuing success in evangelization by Protestant Evangelical and Pentecostal movements across the planet, since they have eliminated clericalism and re-rooted ordained ministry in the *Laos*.

Further, as we have seen, outside Western Catholic Christianity, practically all the other twenty-three *sui juris* Churches of the global Catholic communion never accepted monastic celibacy as mandatory law for diocesan presbyters. They still largely follow the ancient apostolic tradition of allowing married presbyters, if not bishops.

Finally, as we have also seen, the non-evangelical papal law of monastic celibacy for bishops and diocesan presbyters never existed as a broad institutional policy within the Western Church during its entire first millennium.

Bourgeois Captivity of
Late Modern Western Catholic Leadership

Again, the modern Western "clerical-celibate-seminary" model for Catholic presbyters is now breaking down within the 'advanced' industrial countries. That breakdown is revealed by the dramatic "shortage of vocations" and by the often intellectually weak and sometimes emotionally unhealthy quality of many seminarians.[3]

Yet most contemporary Western Catholic bishops still resist understanding the depth of this historical-spiritual breakdown of the modern "clerical-celibate-seminary" model of the Western Catholic presbyterate. They also still resist understanding the relationship of that historical-spiritual breakdown to the wider historical-spiritual breakdown of the modern Catholic evangelization across the Western industrial-center countries.

---

[3] For a reflection on the seminary aspect of this breakdown, see the essay by Alberto Melloni, "*La messa è finita. Così dopo cinque secoli tramonta la figura del prete,*" LA REPUBLICA (Italy), 2017-03-22, available at: *http://ilsismografo.blogspot.it/2017/03/italia-la-messa-e-finita.html* (accessed 2017-03-30). For an English-language article on this essay see Robert Mickens, "Letter from Rome: The Church's Seminary Problem," COMMONWEAL MAGAZINE, 2017-03-27, available at: *https://www.commonwealmagazine.org/letter-rome-117* (accessed 2017-03-30).

Again, according to this analysis, those breakdowns form part of the wider and correlative Western breakdowns of Modern Psychological Spirituality and of Modern Industrial Civilization.

During the nineteenth century, at the end of the Ancien Régime, most European Catholic bishops remained imprisoned in what we might call their "*aristocratic captivity*." They failed to understand the deep spiritual challenges emerging from the bourgeois political economy of the *Modern Industrial Revolution*. In major regions of Western Europe, that caused the massive failure of evangelization known as the "loss of the working class."

Today, across the industrial-center countries of Western Civilization, we see what we might call the "*bourgeois captivity*" of many Western Catholic bishops. Often enmeshed in a corporate-capitalist model of management and networking, many Western Catholic bishops seem blind to the deep historical-spiritual challenges emerging from the *Postmodern Electronic Revolution*.

As a result, another great Western Catholic de-evangelization is now underway, and this time especially across the 'advanced' English-speaking countries of Modern Industrial Civilization.

Breakdown of the
Modern Western Catholic Evangelization

Yet there is no shortage of "vocations" for ordained ministerial leadership within the Protestant Reformation's Evangelical and Pentecostal movements.[4] The reason is that those still growing

---

[4] These churches are different from the "mainline" Protestant denominations, which constructed a deracinated academic professionalism for ministerial leadership. Further, the "mainlines" by and large became culturally accommodated to Modernity, and thus often lack the counter-cultural spiritual energy found in the Evangelical and Pentecostal movements. Further, the "mainline" Protestant

Christian movements rejected for ministerial leadership the non-evangelical model of clericalism, as well as the non-evangelical requirement of celibacy.

In their place, they have embraced *the original lay form of ecclesial leadership*. In addition, many of those pastoral leaders have embraced the Electronic Revolution as a central medium for evangelization.

More importantly, the still globally expanding Evangelical and Pentecostal movements have returned to the ancient Christian tradition of pursuing evangelization, and of discerning ecclesial leadership within evangelization, primarily through *locally-rooted lay kinship and friendship networks*.

In that return, Evangelical and Pentecostal movements frequently ordain local grass-roots leaders, and then often allow them to remain and minister within their local communities – as happened in the original lay movement of Jesus' disciples.

Those contemporary Reformation movements have thus rejected the deracinated and segregated "clerical-celibate-seminary" model for ordained leadership developed by the Catholic papacy across the late classical, medieval, and modern periods. They have also often rejected the deracinated clerical-professional model developed for the "mainline" Protestant Churches, which have typically sought cultural integration with secular modernization.

Consequently, across the globe, Evangelical and Pentecostal movements, and especially Pentecostal movements which empower women, have been dramatically expanding their evangel-

---

churches, at least in the United States, have a different problem. While they do not have a shortage of "vocations" for pastoral ministry, they do have a growing shortage of congregational members to serve.

ization. Of course, such movements often also bring other anti-evangelical problems, like the so-called "Gospel of Prosperity."

Meanwhile, within the 'advanced' industrial-center countries, the deracinated and segregated "clerical-celibate-seminary" model of the Catholic-Christian presbyterate collapses into ever deeper crisis, and sometimes in a pathological manner.

This late modern crisis of the Western Catholic presbyterate within the industrial center-countries remains inseparable from the Western Church's non-evangelical law of "clerical celibacy" for diocesan presbyters and bishops.

Yet changing that papal law will not of itself resolve the late modern crisis of Catholic-Christian evangelization, though such a change is surely a *sine qua non* (necessary pre-condition).

To address the crisis at the deep cultural-spiritual level, there will also need to be a profound transformation in the grounding historical spirituality, as well as a return to the apostolic model of ordaining local grass-roots leaders to the presbyterate without the "clerical state" and without the segregated "clerical-seminary" model of education.[5]

Of course, voluntary evangelical celibacy constitutes an important spiritual charism for those whom the Holy Spirit calls to it. But human-made ecclesial law cannot forcibly impose the Holy Spirit's gift of a special charism on an institutional office. When that happens, there eventually occurs an anti-spiritual distortion of the very nature of that office, as well as an institutional deformation of its spiritual power.

---

[5] On this transformation as the embrace of what Pope Francis has called "ecological spirituality," see again my full book POSTMODERN ECOLOGICAL SPIRITUALITY.

Further, though it is not developed in this small book, my larger book POSTMODERN ECOLOGICAL SPIRITUALITY also argues that the postmodern cultural-spiritual transformation, *in its deep mythic-symbolic foundation,* is moving beyond classical hierarchical patriarchy and beyond modern hyper-masculinism (with both carrying undertows of misogyny), toward an egalitarian and co-creative partnership of feminine and masculine historical-spiritual energy.

For that reason, it is now essential to create across global Catholic Christianity *regenerative postmodern paths that welcome women's pastoral and spiritual leadership.*

4

TWO-STAGE FEUDAL DEVELOPMENT OF
WESTERN MEDIEVAL MONASTICISM

Negative Doctrines from Hellenist Philosophy

While most Christians in the late classical period continued to follow the teachings of Jesus, some Christian teachers contaminated the "Way" of Jesus with negative teachings from certain strains of Hellenist Philosophy.

Such negative doctrines wrongly expressed contempt for material creation, including for the human body, for human sexuality, and especially for the bodies of women (whom Genesis 1:27 describes as the feminine face of the image of God).

Such negative and anti-evangelical teachings, including from extreme versions of Neo-Platonism and Manichaeism, had long circulated across the Hellenistic culture that arose in the wake of the conquests of Alexander the Great (356-323 BCE).[1]

---

[1] For example, Plato, out of whose teachings Neo-Platonism developed, had viewed women's "soul" (*psyche*) as equal to men's "soul" in the spiritual pursuit of wisdom (with "Philosophy," meaning from its Greek roots the "love of wisdom"). Plato had also taught that the human rational "soul" had no gender, but that

The late classical center of Neo-Platonist Philosophy became the North-African city of Alexandria, to which (according to the Coptic tradition) the evangelist Mark had originally brought Christianity, and which later became a Christian "patriarchal" city.

Yet contempt for material creation – again including for the human body, for human sexuality, and for the bodies of women – had never been part of Jesus' teaching.

Although most Christians believe that Jesus lived the spiritual creativity of the celibate vocation and even encouraged select individuals to follow that path, the Gospels make clear that Jesus did not combine his honoring of the charism of celibacy with contempt for material creation, nor for the human body, nor for human sexuality, nor for women.

In stark contrast to demeaning of women by negative strains of Hellenistic philosophy, Jesus held up women as exemplary hearers and proclaimers of the Gospel.

---

genderless rational "souls" had "fallen" into, and become trapped within, human bodies, which then constituted temporary prisons for the entrapped souls. In that corporeal entrapment, however, Plato had defined *the female body as inferior to the male body*, since he ranked it lower than the male body in the descending hierarchy of reincarnation for those who failed to become enlightened philosophers.

Further, the misogyny of Plato's student Aristotle is notorious. In his book POLITICS he wrote that women, as well as 'uncivilized' and 'barbarian' tribal peoples, were sub-human due to an alleged lack of rationality. Aristotle's proof that 'barbarian' tribes were not fully rational was that they viewed women and men as equals. If the 'barbarian' men were equal to 'barbarian' women, Aristotle concluded, then both must be subhuman. That absurd reasoning was also Aristotle's justification for the Greeks hunting "slaves" among the Slavic 'barbarian' tribes (from which we get the name "slaves").

On the deep Western philosophical bias against women found in the writings not only of Plato and Aristotle, but also of Descartes, Rousseau, Kant, Hume, Locke, and Hegel, see Nancy Tuana, WOMAN AND THE HISTORY OF PHILOSOPHY (Paragon House, 1992).

We see this in his mother Mary's special role, in the refusal of key female disciples to flee from his crucifixion, and in his first appearance after the resurrection to Mary Magdalene, who was his most important female disciple.

Yet those negative and anti-evangelical doctrines from certain strains of Hellenistic philosophy would later contaminate the medieval development of Western monasticism in its second stage.

Feudal Emergence
of Western Monasticism

At the end of the West's late classical period, with the growing migrations of 'barbarian' Germanic tribes into the Western Roman Empire, with the migrating tribes' military attacks on Western imperial cities, and with the slow but relentless internal breakdown of the Western imperial organization, the Roman Empire in the West fell into turmoil and decline.[2]

Many historians have judged that, by the end of the fifth century, the Western Empire ceased to exist, though some imperial structures continued beyond that point, and many so-called 'barbarian' tribes integrated Roman traditions into their cultures.

In the wake of the late classical migration of Germanic tribes from the East and the related collapse of the Western Empire, there emerged into spiritual dominance a new Western wave of Catholic-Christian male-celibate energy called "monasticism."

That wave grew in part out of the earlier lay coenobitical communities, which had included both celibate Christians and married

---

[2] The Eastern Roman Empire, known also as the Byzantine Empire and centered in the Greek city of Constantinople (known earlier as Byzantium), survived until its conquest by the Ottoman Turks in 1453.

Christians with families. Medieval male-celibate monasticism, which in the second stage became clericalized, then developed across West Europe into the dominant institutional form of Catholic spiritual energy.[3]

When the migrating Germanic tribes triumphed militarily by plundering Western imperial cities, many Western urban dwellers fled for survival to rural areas where they joined fortified enclaves.

Such enclaves then became the new "feudal" form of Western European society. Decentralized and ruled over by patriarchal-aristocratic warlords, those fortified rural communities bound their members in oaths of fealty to their respective warlords.

Within that new feudal historical context, the new strategic question for visionary-prophetic leaders within the Western Catholic-Christian community became how to evangelize the migrating Germanic tribes, and with them how to rebuild Western Christian Civilization.

The feudal emergence of Western monasticism constituted the strategic response of Catholic spiritual energy to the emerging Western post-imperial feudal challenge.

The feudal development of Western monasticism represented an historically new spiritual-institutional form for Western Catholic Christianity, even though other forms of monasticism had existed earlier within Eastern Christianity and within Eastern Buddhism, and probably as well as within Western Mediterranean Pythagorean communities.

---

[3] For more on this story, see Chapter 4, "Past Long Waves of Catholic-Christian Spiritual Energy," in Holland, POSTMODERN ECOLOGICAL SPIRITUALITY.

First Stage of
Irish-Keltic Monasticism

The migrating Germanic tribes settled in Western rural areas alongside the existing Western tribal peoples, including Keltic tribes which had migrated earlier from Asia Minor.

In response to that new social situation, the Keltic Catholic Church in Ireland sent highly educated and scholarly male monks from the Irish tribes, often the sons of royal or aristocratic families, as nomadic missionaries to convert, and to educate, the migrating Germanic tribes.

Those Irish-Keltic missionary monks soon became strategic partners with converted royal and aristocratic leaders of the Germanic tribes in creating the new medieval form of Western Christian Civilization.[4]

---

[4] Most histories of Western monasticism unfortunately give only a brief and poorly informed account of the great work of the Irish-Keltic evangelization and education of the Germanic tribes in Western Europe.

For a popular account of the intellectual-spiritual role of Irish-Keltic monasticism in evangelizing Western Europe and in regenerating Western Christian Civilization, see Thomas Cahill, HOW THE IRISH SAVED CIVILIZATION: THE STORY OF IRELAND'S HEROIC ROLE FROM THE FALL OF ROME TO THE RISE OF MEDIEVAL EUROPE (Anchor, 1996).

For an older and extensively-researched scholarly analysis of that achievement, see Benedict Fitzpatrick's two magisterial studies, IRELAND AND THE MAKING OF BRITAIN (Funk & Wagnalls, 1922) and IRELAND AND THE FOUNDATIONS OF EUROPE (Funk & Wagnalls, 1927). Both of Fitzpatrick's books (originally planned to be one book) are based especially on Fitzpatrick's extensive research in continental manuscripts written in the Irish language. His second book became the source for what Peter Maurin, co-founder with Dorothy Day of the Catholic Worker movement, called his three-part "Green Revolution."

Scholarly neglect of the powerful impact of Irish-Keltic monasticism in standard histories of Western monasticism may be partly due to their lack of adequate

Benedict Fitzpatrick's magisterial book, IRELAND AND THE MAK-
ING OF EUROPE, states that the Irish-Keltic missionaries were often
sons of royal or aristocratic Irish families.[5] Formed in the great
Irish monastic schools of higher education (perhaps in part a legacy of the ancient Druid intellectual tradition), they carried advanced training in Philosophy, Theology, and the Liberal Arts, including fluency in both Greek and Latin, as well as knowledge of
classical works like the writings of Cicero.

Fitzpatrick also pointed out that from across the British Isles other
Keltic monks, trained in the great Irish monastic schools of higher
education, also participated in the great Irish-Keltic mission to the
migrating Germanic tribes settling in continental Western Europe.

Again, while most Latin Church intellectuals of that time were ig-
norant of Greek (Saint Augustine of Hippo, for example, could
never learn it), the Irish-Keltic scholars carried a long tradition of

---

research into manuscripts in the Irish language. It may also be the result of marginalization of the Irish-Keltic Church by the Imperial Roman Church (similar to
what happened to the "Donatist" African Coptic Church), as well as of the subsequent destruction of Irish manuscripts within Ireland by Viking plundering and
still later by British Protestant imperialism.

Further, Saint Augustine of Hippo (354-430) early on may have laid a theological
foundation for the later marginalization of the Irish-Keltic Christian tradition
across continental Europe, as part of his promotion of the Imperial Church. That
happened especially through his polemic against the Irish-Keltic theologian Pela-
gius, who was his competitor for intellectual-spiritual leadership within Roman
aristocratic Christian circles. (Many contemporary scholars have argued that Pela-
gius was not a "Pelagian.")

Also, some scholars see the evangelization of Ireland by St. Patrick as promoting
the Latin diocesan model at the expense of the traditional Irish-Keltic monastic
model of Christianity, which had been established in Ireland long before Patrick.
In addition, the Roman-directed Synod of Whitby (664) weakened Keltic monasticism in England, in favor of the organizational model of the Latin Benedictine monasticism supported by the Imperial Church.

[5] See the full referencing of this book in the preceding footnote.

fluency in Greek, and they were well schooled in the classical Greek intellectual legacy.

It could be that early Irish-Keltic Christianity was originally closer to the Eastern Churches – including the Syrian and Greek Churches, and perhaps also to the African Coptic Church with its vast coenobitical movement – than to the Latin or Roman Imperial Church.

In addition, the Irish-Keltic scholars' fluency in Greek could have roots in the fact that Keltic tribes had migrated out of the East, where there had been an ancient Keltic presence within the Greek-speaking territories of Asia Minor. For example, in the region that is today's Turkey, the ancient province of Galatia had been Keltic (to whose Church Saint Paul wrote an epistle and with a name similar to the Keltic region of Galicia in Spain,).[6] In addition, a Keltic army once almost conquered Athens.

Fitzpatrick's important book abundantly documents how, by sharing their sophisticated education with leaders of the Germanic tribes across Western Europe, the Irish-Keltic missionaries worked with Germanic tribal leaders to found monasteries, promote sedentary agriculture, build libraries and schools, and establish towns.

For example, Fitzpatrick pointed out that the Austrian city of Vienna still honors the important contribution by Irish-Keltic monks

---

[6] Several years ago, while visiting the Turkish city of Istanbul, my wife and I were delightfully treated to a concert of what was described to us as "ancient Turkish music." To my ears at least, it sounded much like the reels and jigs of traditional Irish-Keltic music from my own Irish-ethnic heritage. Perhaps it was the music of the ancient Keltic presence in Asia Minor.

to its development.[7] He also noted how Irish-Keltic scholars earlier became famous at the Merovingian and Carolingian courts. He even claimed that, centuries later, St. Thomas Aquinas learned about Aristotle, thanks to the work of Irish-Keltic scholars.[8]

While earlier Latin missionaries had failed in their attempt to evangelize the Germanic tribes, the Irish-Keltic missionaries became immediately successful – again, probably because they themselves came from tribal communities and often carried aristocratic or even royal rank.

Thus, according to Fitzpatrick, those visionary Irish-Keltic missionary monks, together with visionary aristocratic and royal leaders of the newly evangelized Germanic tribes, laid the intellectual and spiritual foundations for medieval Europe.

---

[7] The city of Austria was probably originally a pre-Roman Keltic village that was later converted into a Roman fort, and in the eleventh century became an important trading center. In 1055, Henry II of Austria made it his capital and he brought Irish monks to establish a monastery (the *Schottenstift*) for his new city. He required that it be occupied exclusively by Irish monks (*Iroschotten*). In the seventeenth century, however, it became a Benedictine monastery. I recall once visiting that monastery in Vienna and noticing near its entrance a plaque which commemorated its Irish-Keltic foundation.

[8] In IRELAND AND THE FOUNDATIONS OF EUROPE, Fitzpatrick reported:

> *Long after the period of the Irish apostolate the fame of Irish learning lingered in Italy, and in the thirteenth century when the Emperor Frederick II founded the University of Naples, he summoned from Ireland and appointed as his first rector Peter Hibernicus, among whose pupils was no less a personage than St. Thomas Aquinas.*
>
> *Peter was one of a group of Irish literati at the brilliant court of Frederick, where among others resided about the same period Michael the Irishman (Scotus), who learnt Arabic at Toledo and was skilled in Hebrew, and who, with Hermann the German and Andreas the Jew, was instrumental in introducing to Europe several of the philosophical works of Aristotle that before that time had remained unknown in the West. (Page 336)*

Though seldom fully explored in standard Western histories of Christian monasticism, that first Irish-Keltic stage of Western Christian monasticism within Western Europe was the true source for re-founding Western Christian Civilization, after the collapse of the Western Roman Empire.

The Irish-Keltic missionary monastic foundations in Europe were not places where monks left society, but rather places where missionary monks and local tribal leaders worked together to rebuild civilization. Their monasteries became creative centers of spiritual, social, and intellectual regeneration, where Western Christian Civilization could grow anew and with richer cultural diversity.[9]

Meanwhile, in Ireland from which the monks came, Keltic monasticism had long provided stable communities for women and men, as well as for families. Further, in contrast to the Latin model, Irish-Keltic Catholic Christianity, like the original Apostolic Church, celebrated salvation as embracing Nature and welcomed the leadership of strong women. In Ireland, female abbesses reportedly often led closely connected male and female Keltic monasteries.

Therefore, Irish-Keltic monasticism did not accept the negative doctrines from certain strains of Hellenistic philosophy that infected some strains of late classical Latin Christianity. Most importantly, the Irish-Keltic Church cultivated a Nature-rooted ecological spirituality.

---

[9] The late great Welsh Catholic historian and sociologist, Christopher Dawson maintained that the great vitality of European development in the Modern Era was due to its rich cultural diversity that flowed from its early medieval fertilization by the migrating 'barbarian' tribes. See his now classic book, THE MAKING OF EUROPE: AN INTRODUCTION TO THE UNITY OF EUROPEAN HISTORY, Reprint Edition (Catholic University of America, 2002).

In that vein, Irish-Keltic spirituality identified its monasteries not with stone buildings but rather with the beauty of Nature, as in the lush green valley of the ancient Irish-Keltic monastery of Glendalough (Valley of Two Lakes), founded within the gentle Wicklow Mountains during the sixth century by Saint Kevin.

Reportedly, during the so-called European "Dark Ages," thousands of young people came every summer from the European continent to study with the learned Irish-Keltic monks in their lush green monastic valley of Glendalough.

In addition, Thomas Cahill, in his widely read book HOW THE IRISH SAVED CIVILIZATION, claimed that the Irish-Keltic Catholic Church proclaimed the prophetic critique of social injustice as central to the Gospel of Jesus and to authentic evangelization. That would contrast with the late classical Latin Imperial Church, which tended to move away from the prophetic biblical tradition. For example, medieval Roman popes reportedly still held slaves.

Second Stage of
Benedictine Latin Monasticism

In a style different from the heroically nomadic and culturally open mode of Irish-Keltic missionary monasticism, Saint Benedict of Nursia (480-543), son of a Roman noble, developed the second and Latin form of Western monasticism. At the same time, his twin sister Saint Scholastica (480-443) founded the female branch of the order.

Yet Benedict never tried to expand his foundation by missionary outreach to the Germanic tribes. Instead, he provided a classical Latin education for the sons of Roman patrician families. In contrast to the journeying-pilgrim missionary model of the Irish-

Keltic monks, Benedict required that his monks take a vow of stability, which meant they stayed in one place.

Later, however, the male side of Benedict's different model displaced Irish Keltic monasticism in Europe and became the dominant Western European Catholic model. In some cases, as we will see, it became complicit in the restoration of imperial consciousness within the medieval Latin Church.

In that displacement, the Nature-oriented Irish-Keltic stream of Catholic spirituality was forgotten or repressed by the Latin Church. Its Nature-spirituality continued in memory only at the "Keltic fringe" of Western European civilization. It did not re-emerge with spiritual power until the global ecological crisis of the late twentieth century.

Today, Keltic eco-spirituality has re-emerged as an important Western eco-spiritual response to the global ecological crisis that developed out of the deep spiritual errors planted within the sometimes misogynist and generally dualistic hierarchical ground of what became the Western male-celibate-clericalized form of monastic spirituality.[10]

In its medieval dominance, so powerful became the influence of second stage of Benedictine monasticism on the emerging European society that the great German sociologist, Max Weber, claimed Modern Capitalism was an outgrowth of Benedictine monasticism's spiritual-technological rationalization.

In his famous book THE PROTESTANT ETHIC AND THE SPIRIT OF CAPITALISM (1905), Weber argued that Jean Calvin (founder of the Calvinist strain of Protestantism) was the 'father' of modern Capitalism. He also argued that Benedict had been the 'grandfather.'

---

[10] For more on this claim, see analyses later in this book.

Male Benedictine monasteries were originally spiritual centers of egalitarian community, presided over by loving feudal patriarchs called "abbots" (from the Hebrew word *abba*, meaning "father"). As their mission succeeded, however, some Benedictine monasteries, particularly the Western male European Benedictine monastic network of Cluny, became an enormously powerful male feudal political-economic force.

During the 'high' Middle Ages, wealthy monasteries of Cluny's male Benedictine monks deviated from Benedict's original model of sharing together in the tasks of *ora et labora* (prayer and labor). Those tasks became dualistically and hierarchically divided. On one side, Cluny hired lower-class lay workers assigned to do the "*labora.*" On the other side, upper-class "choir monks" devoted themselves to the "*ora.*"

Those monks then also indulged themselves with luxurious lifestyles. That more 'developed' model of Western monasticism not only lost the unitary character of the apostolic church's original Christian *Laos.* It also abandoned its commitment to evangelical poverty.[11]

In addition, the monks of Cluny became clerics and ordained priests. But, in so doing, they tragically disconnected the theology of the presbyterate from its essential pastoral mission, and from its biblical "preferential option for the poor."

---

[11] Centuries later, in Benedictine monastic foundations within the English Midlands, lower-class lay employees also replaced lower-class lay monks as workers. Those wealthy monastic foundations in the Midlands, devoted to the profitable task of raising sheep to obtain wool for textiles, later became "secularized" by King Henry VIII. Still later, that same region became the English seedbed for the modern Industrial Revolution, which began with the textile industry.

Instead, they converted the Eucharist from a communal celebration into an individualized priestly sacrifice, even with "private masses." They also celebrated the Eucharist in symbolic luxury – proclaiming their wealth with silver and gold chalices, sometimes encrusted with jewels, and with expensive silk vestments embroidered with gold.

In those anti-evangelical distortions, the monks of Cluny undermined the evangelical truth of the presbyterate. They not only spiritually placed their monastic form of the presbyterate above the laity, but they also spiritually disconnected it from the laity.

In the Western Catholic Church, the anti-evangelical distortions of Cluny would burden the theology of the presbyterate (and the episcopate) until the Second Ecumenical Council of the Vatican (1962-1965), and for some presbyters and bishops even long after that.

Forgetting Sacred Immanence

In addition, though feudal Benedictine-Latin monasticism included male and female monasteries (with the female side "cloistered"), it did not include the lay sacrament of Christian Marriage.

Further, the dominant male-clericalized-celibate form of monasticism, typified in Cluny, centered itself in a unilateral masculine spiritual symbol of *sacred transcendence*, seeking to rise 'above' Nature – again, with 'lower-class' "lay" employees assigned to deal with the 'lower' tasks of Nature.

As a result, the hierarchical culture of Western Latin male-celibate-clericalized monasticism tended spiritually to forget the first Divine revelation in Nature of the primal feminine spiritual symbol of *sacred immanence*.

Further, since the male-celibate-clericalized form of Benedictine monasticism became in the 'High' Medieval Era the center of Western or Roman Catholic Theology, many leaders of the Western Roman Church theologically over-emphasized *sacred transcendence* as the unilateral masculine symbol of the Divine Mystery. In addition, they implicitly tended to identify the male face of the Divine Mystery with male celibate ordained "clerics."

Finally, in the 'high' Middle Ages, major strains of male-clericalized-celibate monasticism, promoting its male-clericalized-celibate interpretation of transcendence, gained great political-economic power. The rich and powerful Benedictine monasteries of Cluny, after becoming the largest landowner in Western Europe, began to control the papacy. Through the papacy, they then began to pressure the entire Western Church toward what they considered a monastic 'reform' of the presbyterate and episcopate.

5

CRUEL PAPAL ATTACK BY THE
MONASTIC-INSPIRED 'GREGORIAN REFORM'

Misogynist Contempt for Women

I n their 'reforming' zeal for masculine transcendence, the papal
leaders of the "Gregorian Reform," inspired by the rich and
powerful Benedictine monastic network of Cluny, set out to impose an extreme Neo-Platonist anti-sexual model on traditionally
married Western Catholic bishops and presbyters.

In a cruel attack on the Catholic wives and children of traditionally married Western Catholic bishops and presbyters, as well as
on the bishops and presbyters themselves, the popes of the "Gregorian Reform" declared "clerical marriages" to be *heretical.*"

That ridiculous claim became a source of great tension with the
Eastern Churches, which rejected such an absurdity that so clearly
contradicted the New Testament. That ridiculous claim also aggravated the eleventh-century East-West Schism between the
Western and Eastern Churches. Hundreds of years later, it then
contributed to the evangelizing success of the Protestant Reformation, which rightfully rejected the anti-evangelical imposition
of "clerical celibacy."

The long historical drive by fanatical monastic minorities to force a monastic-celibate model on traditionally married Western bishops and diocesan presbyters finally triumphed in the so-called "Gregorian Reform," identified with Pope Gregory VII who was Bishop of Rome in the late eleventh century (1073 to 1085).

Known earlier as Hildebrand and inspired by the Benedictine monasticism of Cluny, Gregory pursued his cruel campaign to force by coercive police-power all Western bishops and presbyters, who had continued the thousand-year old Catholic tradition of episcopal and presbyteral families, *to abandon their Catholic wives and their Catholic children.*[1] A horrendous part of that vicious anti-evangelical campaign was an underlying *misogynist contempt for women.*

The contemporary historian Anne Llewellyn Barstow, in her scholarly book MARRIED PRIESTS AND THE REFORMING PAPACY,[2] has reported that the monastic-inspired "Gregorian Reform" not only removed by police-force the wives of bishops and presbyters from their homes, but often condemned their wives to *homelessness, prostitution, and even suicide.*

With scholarly understatement, Barstow has described that cruel papal attack on the families of Catholic bishops and presbyters as the *"monasticizing of the clergy."*

Further, Anne Llewellyn Barstow and the earlier historian Henry Lea, both distinguished scholars, have stated that written records

---

[1] On this period, see the classic study by Henry C. Lea, HISTORY OF SACERDOTAL CELIBACY IN THE CHRISTIAN CHURCH (Kessinger Publishing, 2003), with the original published in 1867. Lea was at one-time President of the American Historical Society.

[2] Anne Llewellyn Barstow, MARRIED PRIESTS AND THE REFORMING PAPACY: THE 11TH CENTURY DEBATES (Edwin Mellen, 1982).

of resistance by traditionally married bishops and presbyters suggested that there was *a homosexual clerical culture* behind the 'reforming' papal attack on clerical families.

In his celebrated work CHRISTIANITY, SOCIAL TOLERANCE, AND HOMOSEXUALITY, the late distinguished Yale historian John Boswell documented the medieval "clerical" tolerance of homosexuality.[3] Yet it was during this same period of "tolerance" that the monastic-inspired papal attack on the Christian marriages and families of Western bishops and presbyters occurred.

Why tolerance on one side, but not on the other? In response to that question, Anne Llewellyn Barstow has summarized Boswell's honest narrative:

> *The Gregorian church ... in the century 1050-1150 created no legislation against gay clergy. Indeed, it has been argued that this was a period in which homosexuality flourished among clerics, especially in monasteries, and that since monks gained the ascendency in the church at this time, the legislative centers of the church had little choice but to go light on the question of men who loved men.*

> *John Boswell claims that St. Anselm and several of his pupils, Pope Alexander II and Archbishop Lanfranc, Archbishop Ralph of Tours and his beloved "Flora," Bishop John of Orléans, Bishop William Longchamp of Ely, and most notably Ailred of Rievaulx and his Simon all represent influential churchmen whose actions and/or writings help make this century notable for clerical homosexuality.*

---

[3] John Boswell, CHRISTIANITY, SOCIAL TOLERANCE, AND HOMOSEXUALITY: GAY PEOPLE IN WESTERN EUROPE FROM THE BEGINNING OF THE CHRISTIAN ERA TO THE FOURTEENTH CENTURY (University of Chicago Press, 2005.)

Boswell goes so far as to claim that "there was more than a coin-cidental relation between gay sexuality and some of the [celibacy] reforms ... A satire against a reforming bishop specifically ac-cuses him of hostility to clerical marriage because of his own ho-mosexual disposition." There is some evidence of a power struggle between gay and married clergy over whose predilections would be stigmatized. Indeed, we will see that several [medieval] mar-ried clerical authors will express themselves vehemently on just that point.[4]

How sad the apparent medieval battle between "gay" and "straight" "clergy." In that case, for the "clerical" world at least, the "gay" side won, and the non-evangelical legacy of canonically mandatory male "clerical celibacy" became institutionalized in the Latin Church. In the wider society and over longer history, how-ever, "straight" prejudice would inflict vicious hatred on "gay" people. Yet all persons on both sides are our loving Creator's be-loved children, and all persons on both sides bear the sacred im-age of the Creator's beauty and goodness.

Both Barstow and Lea also pointed to *hate-filled misogynist lan-guage* from some leaders of that 'Reform.' The worst-known exam-ples came from Pietro Damiani (c. 1007-1072), a Benedictine monk, later cardinal, still later a declared saint, and at the time lead papal agent of the Gregorian attack on the Catholic families of Western bishops and presbyters.

Damiani's vicious words betray a horrendous contempt for women, and in particular for the female body. As an example, Barstow has cited one of Damiani's many "fulminations" against

---

[4] Barstow, MARRIED PRIESTS, pp. 113-114; Boswell, CHRISTIANITY, pp. 210-227.

the Catholic women who shared in the apostolic tradition of married bishops and presbyters:

> *I speak to you, o charmers of the clergy, appetizing flesh of the devil, that casting away from paradise, you, poison of the minds, death of souls, companions of the very stuff of sin, the cause of our ruin.*

> *You, I say, I exhort you women of the ancient enemy, you bitches, sows, screech-owls, night owls, she-wolves, blood-suckers ... Come now, hear me, harlots prostitutes, with your lascivious kisses, you wallowing places for fat pigs, couches for unclean spirits, demi-goddesses, sirens, witches.*

> *You vipers full of madness, parading the ardor of your ungovernable lust, through your lovers you mutilate Christ, who is the head of the clergy ... you snatch away the unhappy men from their ministry of the sacred altar ... that you may strangle them in the slimy glue of your passion ...*

> *The ancient foe pants to invade the summit of the church's chastity through you ...* **They should kill you.**[5] *(Bold font added.)*

In still other "tirades" against the wives of presbyters and bishops, Damiani repeated his hatred for women:

> *The hands that touch the body and blood of Christ must not have touched the genitals of a whore ... I have attempted to place the restraints of continence upon the genitals of the priesthood, upon those who have the high honor of touching the body and blood of Christ.*[6]

---

[5] Cited by Barstow, MARRIED PRIESTS, pp. 60-61.

[6] Cited by Barstow, MARRIED PRIESTS, pp. 59-60.

Yet Barstow also told a story about how Damiani's own mother, after his birth, had refused to nurse him, and only the intervention of a priest's wife had saved the life of the baby.

*As the infant Peter lay withering away, an angel of mercy came from an unexpected and ... ironic source: a neighboring priest's wife took pity on the starving infant and talked his mother into offering him her breast, thereby saving the life of **the future scourge of priestly families**. (Bold font added.)* [7]

In the misogynist language of that monastic-inspired papal attack on the families of traditionally married Western bishops and presbyters, we see clearly the infection of Western Catholic spirituality by the negative teachings still spreading contamination from certain anti-material philosophical schools rooted in late classical Hellenism. Again, these negative teachings disparaged material creation, the human body, human sexuality, and especially women's bodies.

Anne Llewellyn Barstow further pointed out that ecclesiastical decrees, at both papal and regional levels, ordered that the wives and children of married clerics should be *sold into slavery*.[8] Henry Lea also documented that Pope Leo IX (1049-1054) had ordered *the enslavements of presbyters' wives,* when the couple refused to be separated.

Similarly, Lea noted, Pope Urban II (1088-1099) – another imposer of the 'Gregorian Reform,' founder of the modern papal Curia, and launcher of the first medieval military "crusade" – *ordered*

---

[7] Barstow, MARRIED PRIESTS, pp. 58-59.

[8] Barstow, MARRIED PRIESTS, p. 43. Leo, also a promoter of the power of Cluny, had brought Hildebrand with him to Rome and, according to Lea, dramatically "magnified" the distinction between "clergy and laity." Lea, HISTORY OF SACERDOTAL CELIBACY, p. 154.

'recalcitrant' clerical wives into slavery. Lea also noted that Urban even "offered the wives' servitude as a bribe to the nobles who should aid in thus purifying the Church."[9]

Further, the historian Earl Evelyn Sperry, dating the "beginning of a crusade against the married clergy" to 1049 (first year of Leo IX's papacy) and describing Pietro Damiani as "principal instigator," pointed out:

> A council at Rome decreed that the wives of the clergy should be attached as **slaves to the Lateran Palace**, and bishops of the church were urged to inflict the same punishments upon the wives of priests. (Bold font added.)

In addition, Sperry reported that later the Hungarian Council of Ofen (1279) enacted that the *children* of ecclesiastics should be the *slaves of the church.*" (Italics added.)[10]

Papal Lust for
Theocratic Imperial Power

Ultimately, according to Earl Evelyn Sperry, what stood behind the cruel 'Reform' was the *monastic-inspired papal lust for theocratic imperial power.* Thus, Sperry wrote:

> With the election of Hildebrand to the Papal chair ... a celibate clergy was indispensable to a realization of his views concerning the position of the Pope in the affairs of the world. His theories

---

[9] Lea, HISTORY OF SACERDOTAL CELIBACY, p. 198.

[10] For both preceding quotes, see Earl Evelyn Sperry, AN OUTLINE OF THE HISTORY OF CLERICAL CELIBACY IN WESTERN EUROPE TO THE COUNCIL OF TRENT (Doctoral Dissertation for Columbia University, 1905), pp. 41-43. The author had been a University Fellow at Columbia University and later became a professor of history at Syracuse University.

are clearly set forth in the DICTATUS PAPAE ... *This enunciation of Papal rights ... is tantamount to a declaration that the Pope is the* **autocrat of the church**. *(Bold font added.)*

As to the powers of the Pope in secular affairs, Gregory declared that he might depose emperors, that he might annul the decrees of all earthly authorities, but that no one could annul Papal decrees, and that he was to be judged by no one. [According to] the DIC-TATUS PAPAE ... **all earthly rulers and powers are amenable and subordinate to the pope**. *(Bold front added.)*

Sperry continued:

As spiritual chief of the world, it was necessary that the Pope should have for his agents **a body of men without local attachments and without personal interests** *to which they might sacrifice the welfare of the church. (Bold font added.)*

It was necessary that their powers should be devoted exclusively to defense and aggrandizement of this great ecclesial institution.

To create a body of men with such singleness of purpose, it was also necessary, besides cutting of all personal interest, to **distinguish them sharply from the people they were to rule**. *(Bold font added.)*

The indelible spiritual attributes conferred at ordination accomplished this to some degree, but celibacy was a much more obvious and striking distinction ... [Celibacy would] deprive the clergy of the cares, ambitions and interests which the rearing of a family involves, and it would **isolate them from their fellow men**. *(Bold front added.)*[11]

---

[11] For these and the preceding paragraphs, Sperry, OUTLINE, pp. 26-27.

Henry Lea concurred with this analysis:

> *Hildebrand ... had conceived **a scheme of hierarchical autocracy** ... To the realization of this ideal he devoted his life with a fiery zeal and unshaken purpose that shrank from no obstacle, and to it he was ready to sacrifice not only the [people] who stood in his path, but also the immutable principles of truth and justice ...*
>
> *Such a man could comprehend the full importance of the rule of celibacy, not alone as essential to the ascetic purity of the Church, but as **necessary to the theocratic structure** which he proposed to elevate on the ruins of kingdoms and empires. (Bold front added.)*[12]

Thus, papal leaders and their agents implemented a misogynist campaign against episcopal and presbyteral families. They did so in support of the Gregorian lust for theocratic power. Meanwhile, baptized Catholic wives of bishops and presbyters, their baptized Catholic children, and their baptized and ordained Catholic husbands and fathers, all became tragic victims of the monastic-inspired and misogynist papal lust for theocratic power.

There were other important issues in the 'Gregorian Reform,' especially the debate over lay-investiture and the papal-imperial struggle. Nonetheless, there is no question about the *deep misogyny* and about *the papal lust for theocratic power.*

Finally, there is also no question but that *the so-called "Gregorian Reform" rejected the apostolic tradition of married bishops and presbyters,* which is affirmed by the New Testament and which continues today, at least for presbyters, within practically all the Eastern

---

[12] Lea, HISTORY, pp. 181-182.

Orthodox and Eastern Catholic Churches, as well as within the Western-rooted Protestant Churches.

6

IMPLICATIONS FOR POSTMODERN
TRANSFORMATION OF CHURCH & SOCIETY

Postmodern Renewal of
Monasticism's Regenerative Charism

N either the "Gregorian Reform's" monastic-inspired lust for theocratic power, nor its cruel misogyny, belong to the authentic core of the ancient and still important monastic movement. The vicious Gregorian attack on Catholic episcopal and presbyteral families represented a tragic pathological deformation of the authentic monastic charism.

Fortunately, following the medieval triumph of Cluny-inspired papal theocratic power, the authentic monastic charism re-emerged, especially in the then new Cistercian and Carthusian reforms of the Latin-Benedictine movement.

But those reforms no longer carried the civilization-forming role that had been introduced to the European continent by the Irish-Keltic missionary monks. Also, the Cistercians and Carthusians, in contrast to the earlier coenobitical movement, excluded from their communities the Catholic Sacrament of Marriage and Catholic family-life.

Jumping far ahead to today, it is interesting to note (as mentioned earlier) that the twentieth-century Catholic-Worker prophet Peter Maurin proposed what I have described as *a postmodern lay agroecological new monasticism.*[1]

In Peter's vision, this new lay form of the monastic movement would retrieve *the civilization-building mission* of the early medieval Irish-Keltic missionaries with the Germanic tribes. In addition, and like the late classical coenobitical movement, it would welcome women and men, both single and married, and families with children.

In my earlier and larger book POSTMODERN ECOLOGICAL SPIRITUALITY (again, from which this shorter book has been excerpted and further developed), I have proposed that such a postmodern lay agroecological new monasticism, as envisioned by Peter, needs to become a central component of the global Christian strategic response to *the late modern devastation of life's integral ecology,* across its interwoven natural, human, and spiritual fabric.

According to that book's analysis, that vast natural, human, and spiritual devastation of life's integral ecology is now being inflicted on the evolving creative communion of life by the expanding power of late modern Neoliberalism, with its underlying philosophy of Nihilism.

In addition, I have proposed, this "new monasticism" needs to create *a regenerative agroecological model of university education,* grounded in the ecological wisdom of Nature itself, as well as in

---

[1] See Joe Holland, PETER MAURIN'S LAY ECOLOGICAL NEW MONASTICISM: A CATHOLIC GREEN REVOLUTION DEVELOPING RURAL ECOVILLAGES, URBAN HOUSES OF HOSPITALITY, & ECO-UNIVERSITIES FOR A NEW CIVILIZATION (Pacem in Terris Press, 2015).

ancient indigenous eco-spiritual traditions and those of all world religions, and in the ecological spirituality developed by postmodern visionaries like the late Thomas Berry.

In the spirit of Peter's vision, as I have also proposed, this postmodern lay agroecological new monasticism needs to *recover its eco-spiritual roots in "Mother Earth."* Further, I have proposed that it needs to embrace marginalized people by developing with them agroecological economies.[2]

Finally, I have proposed that this postmodern monasticism needs to *hold together the Sacrament of Marriage and the charism of celibacy* within a co-creative eco-spiritual partnership.

In the first half of the twentieth-century, Peter sketched the original form of his vision as the Catholic Worker's three-part *"Green Revolution."* Again, he looked back to the early medieval Catholic evangelization and renewal of civilization, as developed by visionary Irish-Keltic missionary "scholars" in partnership with visionary leaders of the migrating Germanic tribes.

Although Peter had once been a member of the De La Salle Christian Brothers, he preferred to describe those Irish-Keltic missionaries in lay terms – not as "monks" but as "scholars." Peter saw those lay "scholars" as integrating prayer, study, and agriculture (*"cult, culture, and cultivation"*), and not simply for monks but more broadly for surrounding rural communities.

Further, disillusioned by contemporary universities and even by many Catholic-university professors, Peter called for his lay

---

[2] On this theme, see the excellent and visionary book by Anthony Flaccavento, BUILDING A HEALTH ECONOMY FROM THE BOTTOM UP: HARNESSING REAL-WORLD EXPERIENCE FOR TRANSFORMATIVE CHANGE (University Press of Kentucky, 2016).

monasticism of a "Green Revolution" to create what he called "*agronomic universities.*"

Today, we might describe Peter's lay agroecological new monasticism as "*regenerative ecovillages,*" organically linked to their surrounding rural communities and to "*agroecological universities.*" In addition, Peter saw this new monasticism, like the monasticism of the Middle Ages, as serving the marginalized poor through what he called "houses of hospitality."

Influence on
Modern Science & Technology

The misogynist spiritual infection of some sectors of Benedictine medieval monasticism also contributed indirectly but powerfully to what I have also called in POSTMODERN ECOLOGICAL SPIRITUALITY *the modern hyper-masculine symbolic-mythic pathology.* That pathology, I proposed, lies deep within the mythic-symbolic foundations of Modern Science.[3]

Recent scholarship has shown that Modern Science, again the grounding carrier of the modern hyper-masculine deformation, arose from medieval male monasteries, even though in the early Modern Period it broke beyond that narrow ecclesial framework.

In his ground-breaking study, A WORLD WITHOUT WOMEN: THE CLERICAL ORIGIN OF WESTERN SCIENCE, the late M.I.T. historian of technology David Noble documented the intellectual roots of the modern West's "New Science" in medieval Latin monasticism.[4]

---

[3] See Holland, POSTMODERN ECOLOGICAL SPIRITUALITY, pp. 126-136.

[4] Oxford University Press, 1993.

Noble had been investigating the question of why there was a hyper-masculine deformation in the foundational style of Modern Science, which he saw as leading Western Civilization into its current unsustainable ecological degeneration.

In his research, Noble discovered how the medieval Latin monastic movement became the incubator of Modern Science's hyper-masculine culture. Of course, Noble also found earlier roots of that deformation in the classical Greco-Roman philosophical tradition. But, he argued, medieval Latin monasticism was the immediate source.

Further, with the birth of Modern Science in the late sixteenth and early seventeenth centuries, there also emerged a *Western lay Christian elite,* both Catholic and Protestant, that intensified the late medieval monastic mythic-symbolic deformation with its own misogynist and anti-ecological deformations.

In her indicting study, THE DEATH OF NATURE: WOMEN, ECOLOGY, AND THE SCIENTIFIC REVOLUTION, the distinguished historian Carolyn Merchant (now retired from her professorship at the University of California Berkley) documented that tragic intellectual construction of an underlying misogynist mythic-symbolic foundation for Modern Science.[5]

In particular, Carolyn Merchant showed how the English Calvinist Francis Bacon (1561-1726), considered by many the founding 'prophet' of Modern Science, adopted *a misogynist metaphor, metaphorically linked to techniques of torture,* to describe the 'masculine'

---

[5] Reprint Edition, HarperOne, 1990.

scientific project of forcing 'feminine' Nature to reveal her "divine secrets."[6]

In addition, the French Catholic René Descartes (1596-1650), considered by many the founding 'father' of Modern Philosophy, infamously *justified the 'scientific' torture of living non-human animals through vivisection* by the absurd claim that they were really machines without feeling.

For these reasons, it should not be surprising that, in its concluding techno-scientific and hyper-masculine "climax," the now globalized form of Modern Industrial Civilization is *devastating our garden-planet Earth's integral ecology of life,* across its interwoven natural, human, and spiritual fabric.

As a result, we now discover that the hyper-masculine drive of Modern Industrial Civilization – across both Liberal Capitalism and Scientific Socialism – has been forcing an ecocidal expansion of scientific-technological *production,* by destroying "Mother Nature's" biological-ecological *reproduction.*

---

[6] In addition to her magisterial book The DEATH OF NATURE, Carolyn Merchant's subsequent ISIS article persuasively defended against denying critics her claim that Bacon was using a metaphor linked to torture as the mythic-symbolic ground for the "New Science." See Carolyn Merchant, "The Scientific Revolution and *The Death of Nature,*" ISIS, 2006, 97:513-533.

By the way, the brilliant Irish scientist, theologian, and Anglican priest Alister McGrath, in his otherwise excellent book THE REENCHANTMENT OF NATURE: THE DENIAL OF RELIGION (Doubleday/Galilee, 2002), blithely rejected Carolyn Merchant's claim about Bacon. But, in that book, he could not yet have been aware of Carolyn Merchant's persuasive defense of the claim in her subsequent ISIS article cited above

Medieval Seeds of Modern
Bourgeois Hyper-Masculine Violence [7]

But let us return to the Medieval Period. With Western medieval monastic male-celibate-clerical power misguiding the eleventh-century papacy, the "Gregorian Reform" expanded its papal theocratic power over Western Europe and beyond.

Within that development, high-medieval popes – again, inspired by the powerful Benedictine monasteries of Cluny – also supported great military campaigns to invade the Middle East, and did so in the name of the Gospel.

Those "Crusades" – paradoxically named after the "Cross" (*Crux* in Latin) of the non-violent Jesus – re-opened major commercial trading routes between West and East, which then led to *the rise of wealthy bourgeois classes* within the 'developing' medieval commercial cities.

Centuries later, through its notorious *"Doctrine of Discovery,"* the early modern papacy supported that same hyper-masculine militarized deformation of Christianity in a new and modern genocidal attack on the First Nations of the Americas.[8]

In that same deformed spirit of a hyper-masculine militarized Christianity, Western Christians also inflicted genocidal suffering on the millions of victims of the Atlantic Slave System. Thus were laid the violent hyper-masculine foundations of modern Western bourgeois commercial society, under a Western Christian banner.

---

[7] The adjective "bourgeois" simply means "urban."

[8] See: *http://ili.nativeweb.org/sdrm_art.html* (accessed v2017-09-21).

Further, out of the early modern social 'emancipation' of the late medieval commercial bourgeois classes, there arose still later the modern bourgeois *"secularization" of society.*

Building on Western monasticism's earlier definition of the "lay" world as "secular," emerging modern "lay-secular" bourgeois elites soon destroyed the sacralized hierarchical-aristocratic civilization of Medieval Christendom. In in its place, modern "lay-secular" bourgeois elites constructed – first in liberal-capitalist form and later in scientific-socialist form – what we know today as secularized Modern Industrial Civilization, which is *spiritually, humanly, and ecologically unsustainable.*

That unsustainable form of civilization in its late modern neoliberal globalized form, under which the entire human family now suffers, is based philosophically on what the prophetic British philosopher Alfred North Whitehead named modern "Scientific Materialism." Scientific Materialism does not reverence matter. Rather, *it destroys the material world's integral ecology of life,* across its interwoven natural, human, and spiritual fabric.[9]

In conclusion, we have seen that the late classical clericalizing and 'high' medieval monasticizing of the Western Catholic episcopate and diocesan presbyterate – as well as the early modern Council of Trent's mandating of monastic-like seminaries – all together spiritually and psychologically uprooted Western bishops and diocesan presbyters from the wider Christian *Laos.*

---

[9] Again, the phrase "Scientific Materialism" was introduced by the distinguished British mathematician and philosopher, Alfred North Whitehead (1861-1947). See his now classic work, SCIENCE AND THE MODERN WORLD (Cambridge University Press, 1926). The content was originally presented in his 1925 Lowell Lectures.

That still reigning *clerical-celibate-seminary model* for the Western Catholic episcopate and presbyterate has now become a *degenerative seed,* which indirectly support both the late modern secularization of society and the late modern devastation of the integral ecology of life across our loving Creator's beloved planet Earth.

Undoing that clericalizing, monasticizing, and educationally segregating model for the diocesan presbyterate will prove to be, I propose, a *regenerative seed* for the sustainable development of a future Postmodern Ecological Spirituality, a future postmodern "New Evangelization," and a future Postmodern Ecological Civilization.

ABOUT THE AUTHOR

JOE HOLLAND, an eco-philosopher and Catholic-Christian theologian, explores the global transition to a democratic and regenerative Postmodern Ecological Civilization.

Joe completed his Ph.D. from the University of Chicago in the field of Ethics & Society, which was an interdisciplinary dialogue of Theology with Philosophy and Social Science. At Chicago, he studied Theology with David Tracy, Philosophy with Paul Ricoeur, and Social Science with Gibson Winter. He was also a Fulbright Scholar in Philosophy at the *Universidad Católica* in Santiago, Chile during the last year of the democratic-socialist government of President Salvador Allende, which was overthrown by the murderous dictatorship of General Augusto Pinochet.

Joe is: Emeritus Professor of Philosophy & Religion at Saint Thomas University in Miami Gardens, Florida, and Adjunct Professor in its School of Law; Permanent Visiting Professor at the Universidad Nacional del Altiplano in Puno, Peru; President of Pax Romana / Catholic Movement for Intellectual & Cultural Affairs USA, and Editor of its Pacem in Terris Press, with both based in Washington DC; Vice-Chair of Catholic Scholars for Worker Justice, with offices in in Boston, Massachusetts; and a member of the International Association for Catholic Social Thought, based at the Catholic University of Leuven in Belgium.

Earlier, Joe served for 15 years as Research Associate at the Washington DC Center of Concern, created jointly by the international Jesuits and the US Catholic Bishops to work with the United Nations on global issues. Later, he taught at New York Theological Seminary in New York City, at the Theological School of Drew University in Madison, New Jersey, and at the Florida Center for Theological Studies in Miami, Florida.